# DAG AND SCOUT'S MULTILINGUAL COLOR BOOK

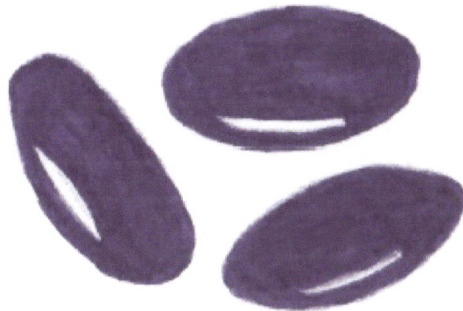

### Sheila Y. Hilton

**zoomzuum**™
Where Imaginations Shop

Title ID: 9239386
ISBN No.: 978-0578425610

Sheila Y. Hilton has a BA in International Studies from New York University and an MIA in International Relations and International Banking and Finance from Columbia University. She was inspired to write her first children's book, Counting Beans with Dag and Scout: a Multilingual Counting Book for Children as a tribute to the multilingual children and godchildren of her dear friends.

Sheila lives in New York City but can frequently be found exploring cities around the world.

# INTRODUCTION

Dag and Scout love to play with Jelly Beans and enjoy counting them in different languages. They found the game of counting Jelly Beans in different languages so much fun that they decided to learn colors in eight languages.

Dag and Scout are twins. Dag is a boy and Scout is a girl.

Dag and Scout would love to invite you to join them and their friends in learning the name of colors in:

English, French, Spanish, German, Italian, Portuguese, Swedish and Mandarin Chinese.

Have fun.

Dag and Scout.

# COLOUR - ENGLISH

black

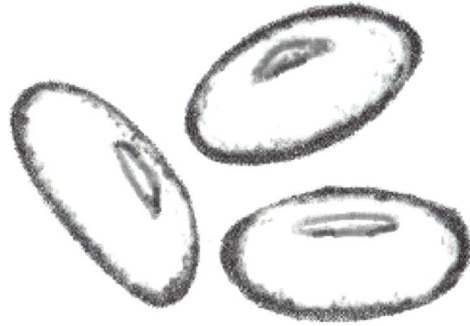

white

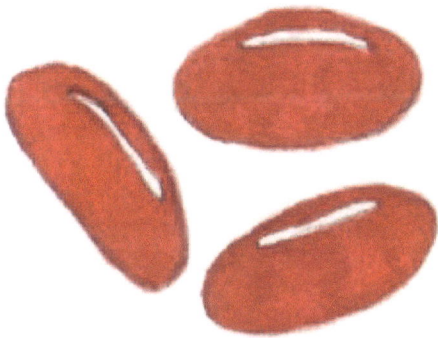

red

blue

# COLOUR – ENGLISH

green

yellow

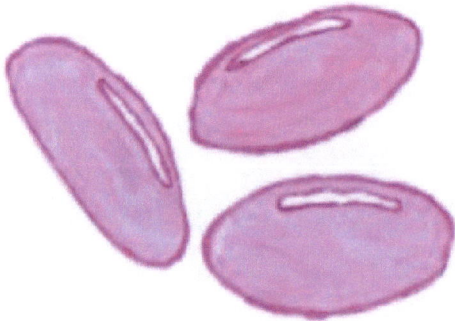

pink

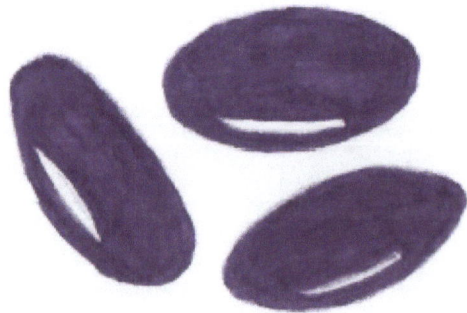

purple

# COLOUR - ENGLISH

brown

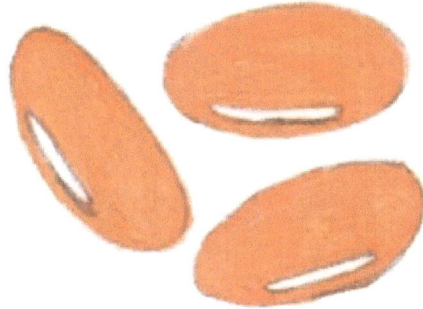

orange

grey

# COULEUR – FRANÇAIS

**noir**
**(nwahr)**

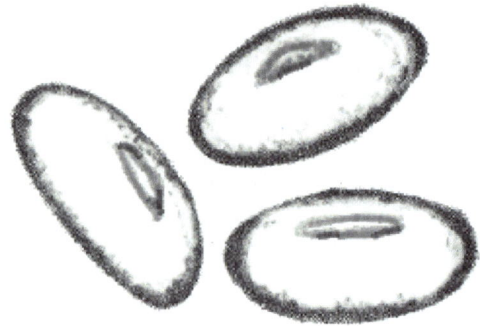

**blanc**
**(blahN)**

**rouge**
**(roozh)**

**bleu**
**(bluh)**

# COULEUR – FRANÇAIS

**vert**
**(vehr)**

**jaune**
**(zhon)**

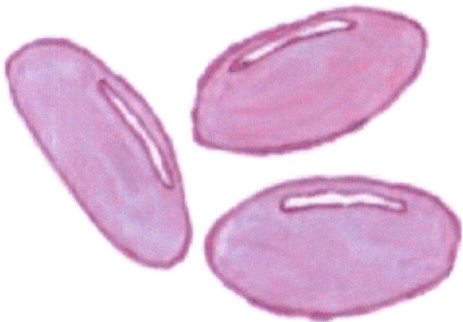

**rose**
**(roz)**

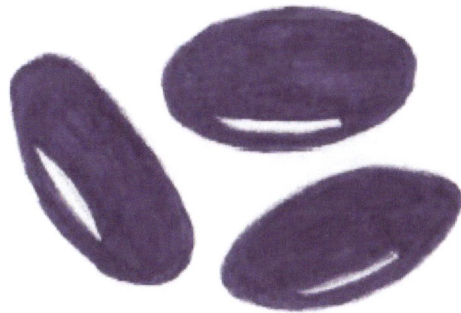

**mauve**
**(mov)**

# COULEUR – FRANÇAIS

**marron**
**(mah-ROHNG)**

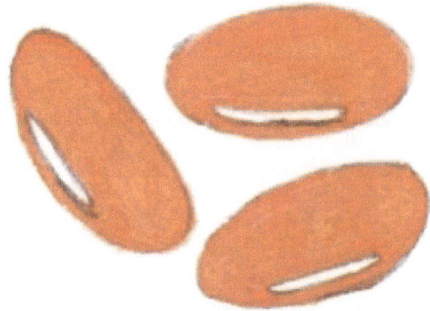

**orange**
**(oh-rahNzh)**

**gris**
**(gree)**

# COLOR - ESPAÑOL

## negro
**(NAY-groh)**

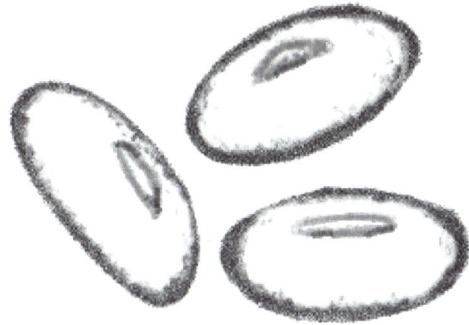

## blanco
**(BLAHN-koh)**

## rojo
**(ROH-hoh)**

## azul
**(ah-SOOL)**

# COLOR – ESPAÑOL

**verde**

**(BAYR-day)**

**amarillo**

**(AH-mah-REE-yoh)**

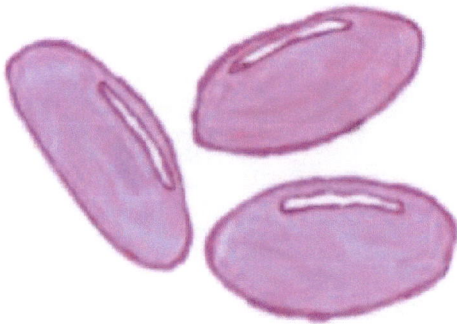

**rosa**

**(rrosa)**

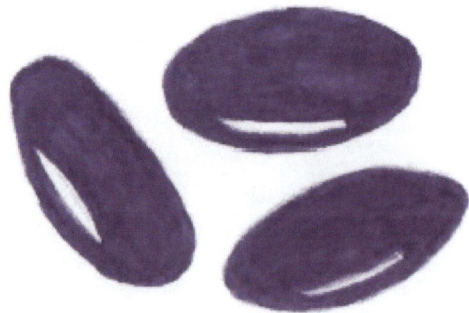

**púrpura**

**(POOR-poor-ah)**

# COLOR – ESPAÑOL

**marrón**
(mah-RON)

**naranja**
(nar-AHN-hah)

**gris**
(GREESS)

# FARBE – DEUTSCHE

## schwarz
**(shvahrts)**

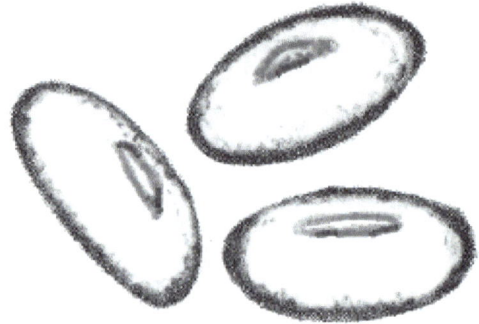

## weiß
**(vighss)**

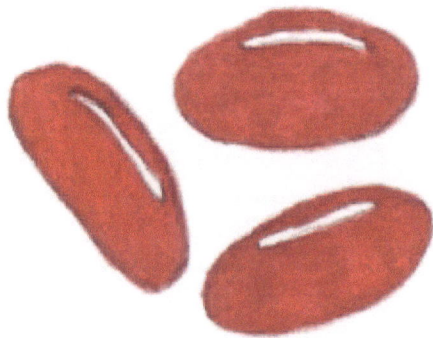

## rot
**(rhot**

## blau
**(blou)**

# FARBE – DEUTSCHE

## grün
**(gruun)**

## gelb
**(gelp)**

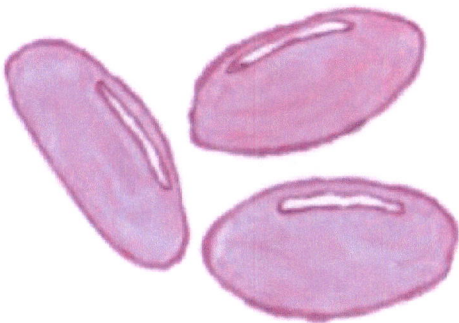

## rosa
**(ROH-zah)**

## lila
**(LEElah)**

# FARBE – DEUTSCHE

**braun**
(brown)

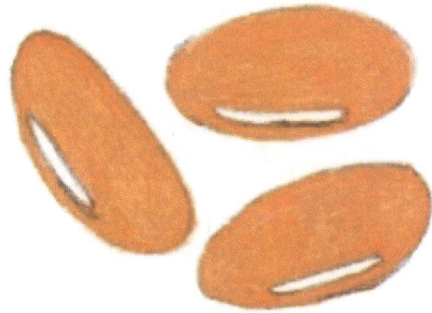

**orange**
(oh-RAHNGSH)

**grau**
(grou)

# COLORE - ITALIANO

## nero
(neh-roh)

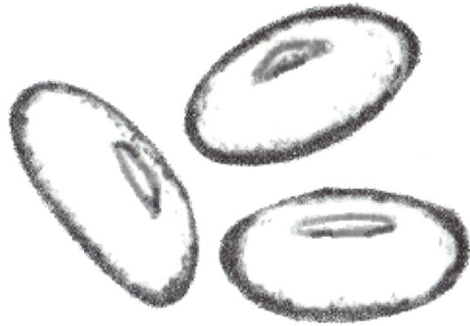

## bianco
(bee-ahn-koh)

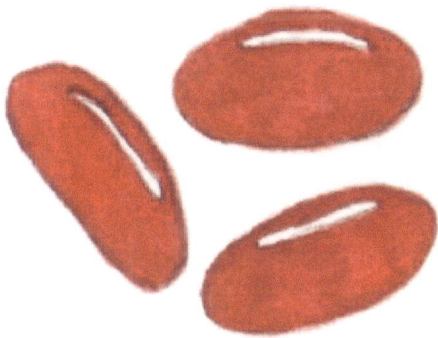

## rosso
(roh-soh)

## blu
(bloo)

# COLORE - ITALIANO

**verde**
(ver-deh)

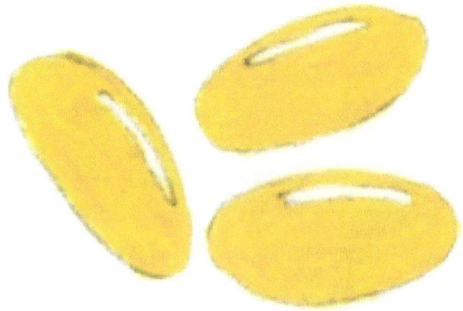

**giallo**
(jahl-loh)

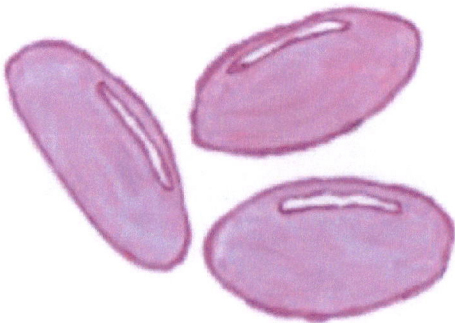

**rosa**
(roh-zah)

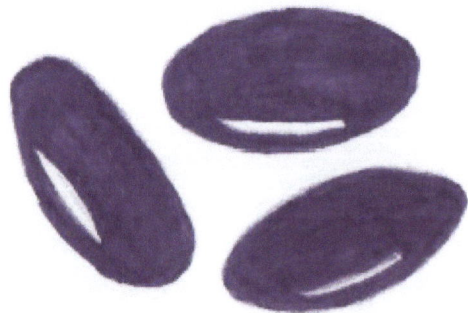

**viola**
(vee-oh-la)

# COLORE - ITALIANO

**marrone**
(mah-roh-neh)

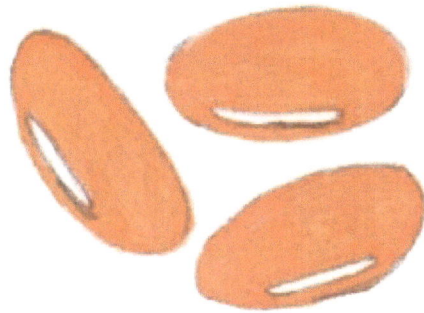

**arancione**
(ah-ran-choh-neh)

**grigio**
(gree-joh)

# COR – PORTUGUÊS

**preto**
(PREH-too)

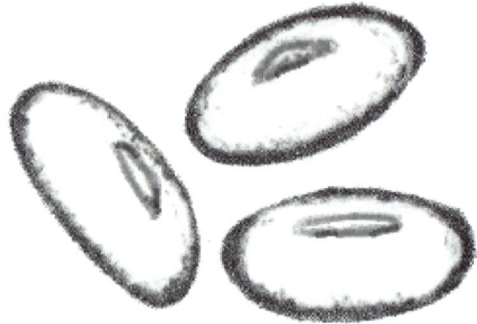

**branco**
(BRAHNG-koo)

**vermelho**
(ver-MEH-lyoo)

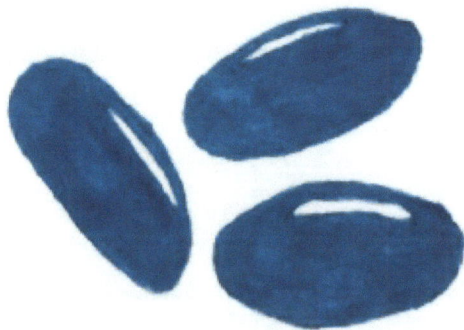

**azul**
(ah-ZOOL)

# COR – PORTUGUÊS

## verde
**(VEHR-deh)**

## amarelo
**(ah-mah-REH-loo)**

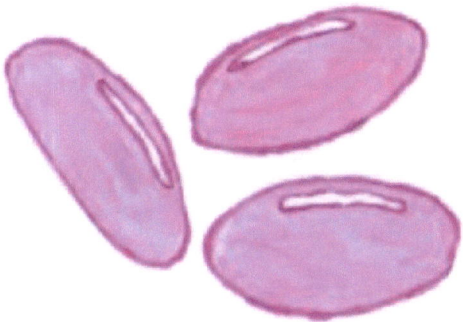

## rosa
**(HOH-sah)**

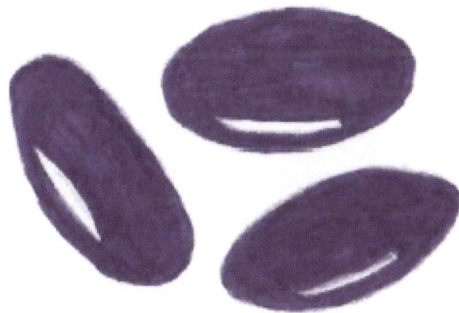

## roxo
**(HOH-show)**

# COR – PORTUGUÊS

**marrom**
(mah-hone)

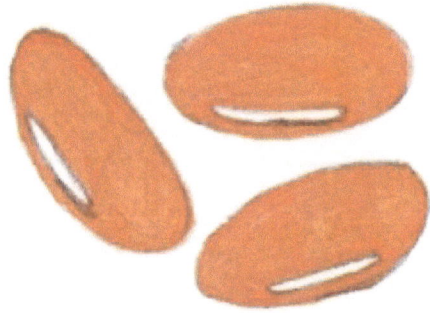

**laranja**
(lah-RANG-jah)

**cinza**
(seen-sah)

# FÄRG – SVENSK

**svart**
(svaahrt)

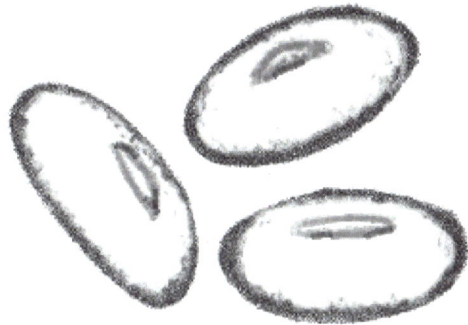

**vit**
(veet)

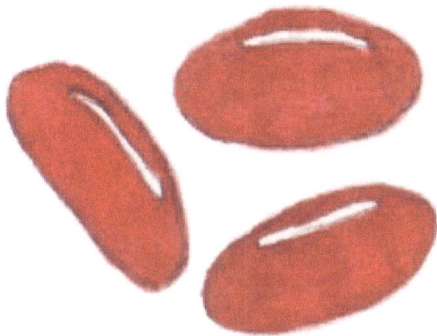

**röd**
(rud)

**blå**
(bloo)

# FÄRG – SVENSK

**grön**
(grun)

**gul**
(gool)

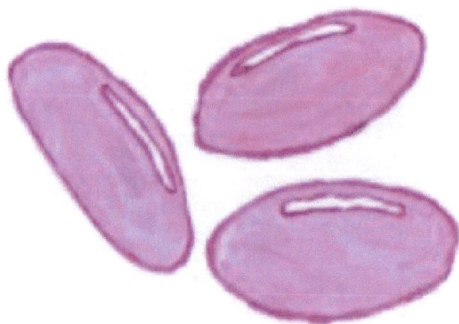

**rosa**
(rooSa)

**lila**
(leela)

# FÄRG – SVENSK

**brun**
**(broon)**

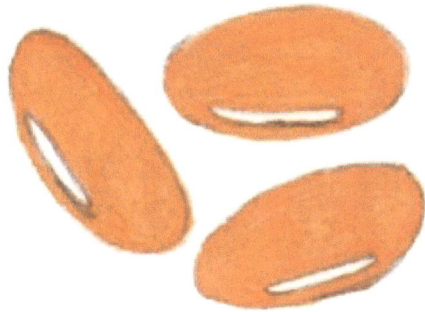

**orange**
**(o raunch)**

**grå**
**(groo)**

# YÁN SÈ - MANDARIN

## hēi sè
黑色
(hey se)

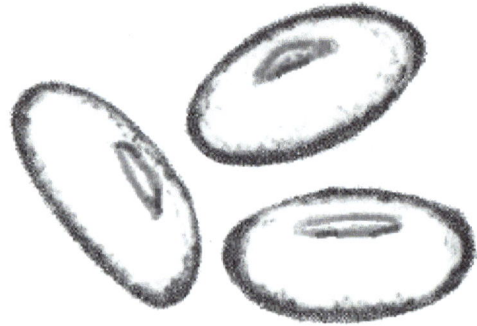

## bái sè
白色
(bye se)

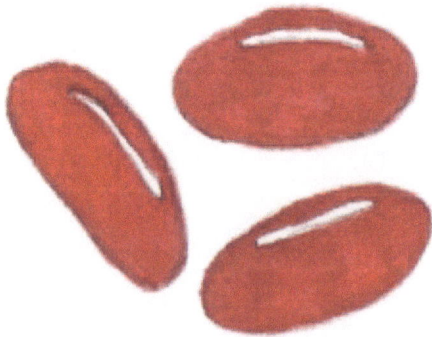

## hóng sè
红色
(hung se)

## lán sè
蓝色
(lance se)

# YÁN SÈ – MANDARIN

## lǜ sè
绿色
(loo se)

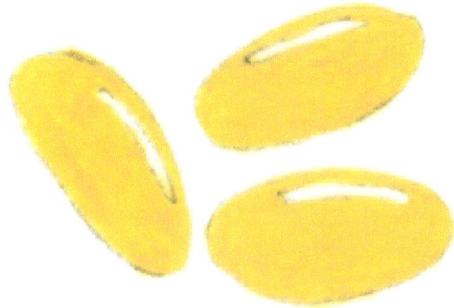

## huáng sè
黄色
(whang se)

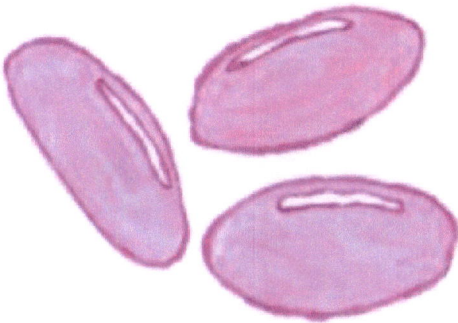

## fěn hóng sè
粉红色
(feng hung se)

## zǐ sè
紫色
(tse se)

# YÁN SÈ – MANDARIN

**zōng sè**

棕色

(sung se)

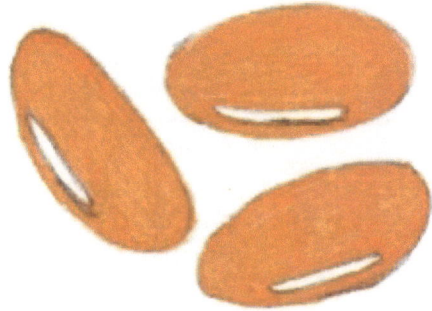

**chéng sè**

橙色

(chung se)

**huī sè**

灰色

(whey se)

www.ingramcontent.com/pod-product-compliance
Lightning Source LLC
Chambersburg PA
CBHW041223040426
42443CB00002B/70